The H
Ca   ore

Uebert Angel

Table of Contents

Chapter 1
The Day God revealed the Prayer
he can't Ignore 5

Chapter 2
The day God got Disturbed! 21

Chapter 3
The Prayer of an Unbeliever 35

Chapter 4
The Day God chose Satan
over his people 48

Chapter 5
Counterfeit Prayer 59

Chapter 6
Robbing God 65

Chapter 6
The 419 Sacrifice 77

Chapter 6
Obedience Better than Scarifice 84

Chapter 1

The Day God revealed the Prayer he can't Ignore

"I do not answer prayer; I have never answered prayer and I will never answer prayer"

'What?' I asked shocked out of my wits. For years, I have been given the grace to speak to the Lord as Moses spoke to him in the days of old, **'as a man speaks to his friend',** but this was a different conversation.

"Prayer is just a medium of exchange to me, I only answer what backs it. I don't answer prayer"

He continued.

With three university degrees in the field of business and finance, the moment I heard the words **'prayer is just a medium of exchange',** my mind raced uncontrollably trying to link the word of the Lord on prayer to what the financial world taught me about mediums of exchange. I knew I was onto something deep but so simple that even a child would get it, but at the time of hearing this I was immediately thrown into discovery mode. I knew right away that I needed to know what makes prayer catch the undivided attention of

God. This was a mission I was not to fail. I just had to know **'the prayer that God cannot ignore!'**

Prayer as a medium of exchange

I knew what a medium of exchange was so when God said;

"Prayer is just a medium of exchange to me, I only answer what backs it. I don't answer prayer".

I was a little shaken because in all my prayers I never had the mind to employ them as mediums of exchange.

I know you might be thinking, what is Brother Angel talking about? Just stay with me on this line and you will be shocked and changed with this revelation, and I assure you after you hear the revelation your prayer life will be sweet because results will start coming.

Now I want to first explain what Money as a medium of exchange does in the economies of the world so as to give you a better understanding of what a 'medium of exchange' is WITH REGARDS TO PRAYER.

Money As a Medium of Exchange

Money, in and of itself, is nothing. It can be a shell, a metal coin, or a piece of paper with a historic image on it, but the value that people place on it has nothing to do with the physical value of the money. Money derives its value by being a **medium of exchange,** which means that money is simply a unit of measurement or a storehouse for wealth or value. Money allows people to trade goods and services indirectly.

Money is valuable merely because everyone knows that everyone else will accept it as a form of payment, but in and of itself it has no real value because it simply represents value that people agreed on, or as in some economies money is backed by gold which in finance is called the gold standard. So since people cannot carry gold around, those economies decided to use a representation of that gold in paper form and that's what we call money. You see its simple a stand in!

It is simply a representation of the real value that we can't carry around. Prayer then as a medium of exchange is simply a representation of real value that is kept somewhere else. So without that value it represents, your prayer is not worth anything. It's just like singing;

"Twinkle, twinkle little star how I wonder what you are"

…and expect God to respond with something.

That will never happen. Why? Because prayer is a medium of exchange to God. It needs to have a certain value outside of it, that makes it a real force.

Real-life Example

Many years ago, a country in Africa called Zimbabwe adopted what they called 'bearer's cheques' to replace their crumbling currency. It seemed to have been a good idea in the eyes of whosoever planned it, but the truth of currencies in a nutshell is that if there is no demand, the economy is not growing enough to give value to the paper you call currency. If there is no value behind the paper you are giving people, you will still have the same issues even if you change the shape, colour, quantity or quality of the paper you call currency. You can even change the name but if factors of value demand and economy are not addressed your currency will simply be a paper with no value. Just a worthless paper.

In the same vein, some prayers that are going forth are simply 'bearer's cheques' in the realm of the spirit. They are simply valueless papers with a 'value' written on them and a quality paper used but it's never a medium of exchange. It has no value to represent. It's that simple. All it is carrying are the list of demands or requests that you are presenting but no backing whatsoever.

See, your prayers can simply be a useless paper that cannot be accepted in the spiritual world as currency, just like the bearers check was only accepted in Zimbabwe and once you stepped out of that country it was not recognised elsewhere. Even in the same country some didn't accept it and the government ended up scrapping it altogether, only to take on the United States dollar as the currency for some time because that had value.

Notice that money, in some form, has been part of human history for at least the last 3,000 years. Before that time, it is assumed that a system of bartering was likely used. Let me explore this for a little to help you understand where I'm going.

Bartering is a direct trade of goods and services. For example, I would give you an axe if you help me kill hunt for an elephant. You see I would have to find someone who thinks an axe is a fair trade for having to face the an elephant. If that didn't work, I would have to alter the deal until someone agreed to the terms. One of the great achievements of money was increasing the speed at which business, whether elephant hunting or building, could be done.

Slowly, a type of prehistoric currency involving easily traded goods like animal skins, salt and weapons developed over the centuries. These traded goods served as the **medium of exchange** even though the unit values were still negotiable.

This system of barter and trade spread across the world, and it still survives today on some parts of the globe. The other problem with barter trade was I would have to find a person who liked what I had to offer, and having something that they also wanted to offer in return. We needed a match yet money as a medium of exchange gives us an ability to use for the goods that have a value written on the paper or coin I am holding.

Prayer is the same. It removes barter trade in the things of the spirit but contains value and that value is stored somewhere else. This is why even 1 John 3:18 says;

"Dear children, let us not love with words or speech but with actions and in truth"

You see, even love has to be backed by something. There is a value that needs to back prayer for it to work. Many believers are ignorant of the fact that the presence or absence of value that is somewhere outside of prayer gives it its value, and not the words inside the prayer. This is the reason why God said to me;

"I do not answer prayer; I have never answered prayer and I will never answer prayer. Prayer is just a medium of exchange to me, I only answer what backs it. I don't answer prayer"

Back to Prayer

So much of the time we treat prayer like we are rubbing a magical lamp and asking the genie inside for our wishes to be granted. Even mature believers often fall into the trap of treating God like some kind of cosmic concierge, who is there at our beck and call to fulfil our every whim and desire when we utter some words in some order. However, the truth is it's not the words or how we sign out our prayer, it's all about understanding prayer as a **medium of exchange** and that it needs a backing of some sort.

This book is the answer to how you can have your prayers answered by learning to back them up by something that makes it a legitimate currency to God. Without the revelation in this book take yourself as an economy suffering a great depression with inflation beating your currency from all angles, or if you like as a person trying to use fake money to buy from a legitimate shop.

There is a prayer that God cannot ignore. Many times, we use the revelation that says you pray then ACT on your prayer yet there are some prayers that you ACT then pray.

When God answers prayer he is responding to more than just the mere words you spoke in prayer, watch this;

Isaiah 65: 24
And it shall come to pass, that before they call, I will answer; whilst they are yet speaking, I will hear.

Now notice here, that God is telling us that before your knees hit the floor to pray, before you even open your mouth to cry out to him, He says I will answer. How can he answer when you have not called? If he is now answering before you call, then what he is answering is no longer the words you are speaking in prayer because you will have not spoken them at that time. He is now responding to something else that gets to him before you pray.

There is now something else demanding an answer before you even pray. No wonder on the day that he appeared to me he said; ""I do not answer prayer; I have never answered prayer and I will never answer prayer", I immediately remembered his words;

"Prayer is just a medium of exchange to me, I only answer what backs it. I don't answer prayer".

He is now answering in response to something more than mere words, that thing has the muscle to arrest his attention before you say anything in prayer. In this case the words themselves have not even been spoken in prayer, yet God is declaring that he will answer an **'unprayed'** prayer. That shocked me to the core.

I was just as puzzled as you are right now until the Lord said to read 1 Kings 3: 5.

1 Kings 3: 5
At Gibeon the Lord appeared to Solomon during the night in a dream, and God said," Ask for whatever you want me to give you."

Look at this carefully, the Lord's visit to Solomon seems unwarranted. Solomon had not named a single prayer request, yet God showed up in the middle of the night to answer a prayer that had not been sent.

If you read from the beginning of that chapter you will not find a single prayer request that Solomon made. This was not normal, think about it, whatever Solomon was going to ask for, God had already made up his mind that he was going to give it when he said;

"Ask for whatever you want me to give you."

This was a blank check. Solomon could have asked for a pink elephant and that is exactly what he would have received. Before the words to utter in prayer had even come to Solomon, God was at his doorstep with the answer to an **'unprayed'** prayer, this was an unsaid prayer.

There was something Solomon had done that got the attention of God and demanded an answer to a prayer he had not even thought of. If you look carefully at the scripture it seems as if there was urgency about the way God came to Solomon that night to say, I need to give you whatever you ask for and I will do it. Solomon had not said a single word in prayer but there was something he did, that went and presented itself before the throne of God demanding an answer to a prayer he had not yet said.

Solomon had secured an answer before asking, or performing the ritual you call prayer. So what God was responding to cannot be his words, he had not prayed! It had to be something else that has the ability to give value to his words in prayer.

This is exactly why God would boast in His ability to perform that which we have not even thought of but it's a realm that very few have touched.

Ephesians 3: 20
Now unto Him who is able to do exceeding abundantly above all that we ask or think, …

Why on earth would God even tell us of His ability to do for us those things that we have not asked, thought about or even imagined? It is because there is a way for you to tap into that level, where God responds to you with answers to prayers you never prayed. That is the prayer we call '**The prayer that God can't ignore**'.

Now I want us to look at Isaiah 65 with that understanding.

Isaiah 65: 24
And it shall come to pass, that before they call, I will answer; whilst they are yet speaking, I will hear.

The Hebrew translated as **answer** in verse 24 of Isaiah 65 is *"anah"* it literally means, to pay attention in order to respond. Notice the second part of that verse says; *"while they are yet speaking, I will hear."* The Hebrew word translated as **hear** there is *shama* it means to hear intelligently or consider. This is different from the first word '*anah*', when God says I will answer that word means the response is guaranteed but when he hears it or *shama* he is considering the request and hearing intelligently. The two are not the same, the first one *anah* guarantees the answer the second *shama* hears and considers the matter with no promises.

When God uses *shama* the merits of you as the 'prayee' are now considered but there are things that cut that out. If I went before the Lord today with a list of my needs like this, he would have to go back and check first of all, who are you, do you tithe or do you even believe this thing is possible, do you do this or that? But if what I am presenting is not just a mere request but is backed up by a currency then it doesn't matter who I am and my character is not in question here, or let me just shock you; your religion may not even matter with this type of prayer. The only thing that now qualifies me is the value of the currency that I am presenting. I will prove to you later!

Merit vs The Prayer That God Can't Ignore

If I went to America with my US dollars when I go shopping they are not going to be asking; 'is your mother Jewish or where do you come from?' No! They won't ask those questions, the US dollar that I will be holding satisfies all their requirements by itself. They accept it only on the basis that it's US dollars that I am holding with the value that it has somewhere. They accept it based on its own merits. It has nothing to do with who I am or where I am coming from. My affiliations don't count.

Now if I get there with a Zimbabwean bearer's check, which has nothing backing it, they are going to be telling me that *"look, we can't accept this here it's nothing personal but brother we don't know what this worthless paper is and we won't accept it".* On the other hand, if I take a currency that is internationally recognized that means it has a value that everybody accepts, they will accept it. That is why you can go to Australia on holiday and exchange your British pounds for Australian dollars, they recognize the value of your British pounds so they will gladly exchange them for their own currency.

Imagine if I just walked into a bakery in town and asked for bread with no money, they will have to point out the fact that this bread is for sale, they are not giving for free. Then if I tell them that my father is the founder of the shop, it now becomes a process of them making phone calls to verify who I am, and whether or not I should be given this bread. They now need verification upon verification before I can even get this thing.

So if you are just going there in prayer with no valuable currency you now need to go through the process of verification before you can receive anything, and there are no guarantees that you will get what you are asking for. Your merits now come into play, this is exactly what happens in prayer when you fail to present a valuable medium of exchange. If all you are doing is speaking words in prayer that have no backing you need a lot of merit, do you tithe and are you in church every Sunday since you say you love God? So there is only one area where your merits don't count but the merits of the thing that backs your prayer counts.

I know I preach the good news of God's grace so it might confuse people why I am on this line that seems like it's a works centred revelation, but listen even grace is obtained by faith and faith is an act but also faith is currency by which to get grace. The only thing is he gives the faith as a gift.

Now you see, faith is a merit and whether or not you are a Christian also counts when it comes to God considering your answer to prayer. Remember the Ephesians 2:8

"For by Grace are you saved through faith…"

You should understand that by supplying us with the thing that backs prayer, God is in his right place as a grace driven God because this is his way of eliminating merits and making everyone have a shot at answered prayer whether they meet the requirement or not. Boy I love Jesus!

I know it goes against everything you have been learning since Sunday School but stick with me we are about to go deeper.

1 Peter 4: 8
And above all have fervent charity among yourselves; for charity shall cover the multitudes of sin.

Watch this, the bible tells us that your giving has the ability to cover a multitude of sins, just by you giving God turns around and says as for your sins they are forgiven. What have you really done? You have just given and God says that's good enough to cover your sins. He accepts your charity as something with the ability to free you from that condemnation.

Now on the other hand you can just pray for forgiveness, but when you do this you must also believe that God will answer that prayer, your faith now comes into play. Notice it's no longer as straight forward as the first, now we have to examine you the one who is praying for forgiveness first. Do you believe this thing and have you also forgiven those that need your forgiveness? Immediately the whole thing shifts and becomes all about you. Do you also forgive others?

Stay With Me On This...

If you went to buy a television today and you take your money with you, you will get there and all will be pretty much straight forward save for the moment you change and say you now want it on credit.

They will need to see your proof of address, credit check and every place you have lived at in the last five years, even your mother's name they will want to know, why? You have not presented the right **'medium of exchange'** and now everything is riding on your **merit** and when things ride on your merit you have to tick all the boxes for you to get what you want. You have to cross every 't' and dot every 'i'. It's that difficult.

You see as aforementioned, in credit applications, your personal history and even your mother's maiden name is required. They are looking for merits to qualify you for the credit. When you buy with your US dollar they look at the value of those US dollars and that value has nothing to do with you or your merit. They know the value and even if you are a murderer that value of the US dollar in your pocket doesn't change. Why? Because it's given value by something that is outside of your character and merit.

Same with *the prayer that God cannot ignore.* When you use it as I will teach you in chapter two onwards, your merit doesn't matter. It's not even considered and no one will ever ask for it. What matters in the prayer that God cannot ignore is the value that backs you medium of exchange.

This is why he said;

"I do not answer prayer; I have never answered prayer and I will never answer prayer. Prayer is just a medium of exchange to me, I only answer what backs it. I don't answer prayer"

You see there are a lot of people who have used this prayer that God cannot ignore to their advantage whilst the average Christian is trying to go before the throne based on merit.

Check out in chapter two what happened when a non-Christian arrested the attention of God and God got disturbed from his daily routine by **The prayer that God can't ignore!**

Chapter 2

The day God got Disturbed!

Do you know there is a day in heaven, where God's direct view of all the beauty of his creation was obstructed by something, so much so that he could not do anything but respond to this intrusion?

Heaven on that day was invaded by something so spectacular that even the translators of the bible didn't quite capture the scene well. It was so intrusive that God himself had to respond to what was in front of Him, something blocked His view, it prevented him from seeing what was in front of Him and stopped Him dead in his tracks from going about his normal routine.

Now you might say 'but God is all powerful so it can't be' but remember that an all-powerful God has made rules that bind Him to certain levels of control. He bound himself to his own word. He cannot oppose it although he has the power to. He himself said;

"I will not alter nor change the word that has gone out of my mouth" Psalm 89:34

He also says he is a servant of his own word so when you use his word you 'force' his hands so to speak. He is bound by his word. This is the reason why I used the subtitle 'how to 'force' God to answer every prayer every time' I used that subtitle to provoke religious spirits in people who call themselves believers. However, my real intention was to show them that God is bound by his word not that anyone has power to force him. No, that can't happen but his word binds God!

Notice this scripture;
"He has exalted his name above every name and his word above his own name" Psalm 138: 2

Do you see that? God himself is controlled by his own words yet he is powerful enough to release himself from such. But because he is also all truth and all faithful he made himself abide within the rule that he won't oppose or alter his word. So, on this day something happened that was so in line with his own word that he stopped dead in his tracks and had to attend to it. As aforementioned, that's why in the subtitle of this book I put a controversial word that I knew would trouble religious people. I put the word 'force' God in inverted comas so as to say there needs to be some connotation.

Back to the Day That God Was Disturbed

Now let me show you someone who worked this same principle and turned around even what the apostles believed about salvation. Cornelius was one of fallen mankind, sinful and condemned before God as all others, yet God accepted his prayers and his alms. The prayer of Cornelius had the ability to arrest God's attention yet he was not even born again. To some this was scandalous, how could God answer the prayer of one who had not even received Christ?

Notice at this point in time Jews were not allowed to share meals with the Gentiles under any circumstances. They were considered unclean according to the Law of Moses. Now for the same God in heaven who gave them those laws, to answer the prayers of a gentile was simply unthinkable, there was no room for that kind of thing.

But Cornelius was not just praying, his prayer became more than mere words that someone recites everyday as a cry for help, no! His words demanded to be heard and compelled heaven to pay attention. There was something different about the prayer of Cornelius, hold on to your seat because what I'm about to show you will blow your mind.

Acts 10:3 and 4 says,
"He saw clearly in a vision about the ninth hour of the day, an angel of God coming in to him and saying to him, Cornelius! And looking intently at him and becoming terrified, he said, What is it,

Lord? And he said to him, Your prayers and your alms have ascended for a memorial before God."

The angel of God said to him; "your prayers **and** your alms are come up for a memorial before God."

The Greek word translated as *'and'* in that passage of scripture is *'kahee'* which literally means **then,** or **mother of**. In other words, we could read the same scripture as; 'your prayers *then* your alms have ascended for a memorial before God.' The angel referred to the prayer of Cornelius as the prayer which gave birth to God looking at what backs his prayer. This is simply saying 'your prayers gave birth to an attitude in God that made him look at your value behind your medium of exchange!

The angel was pointing to the fact that when Cornelius prayed, his sacrifices would not allow his prayer to go unnoticed.

Before God in heaven it was as if a huge flag was being waved in his face and it would not go away until that prayer had been answered. It was as though a statue was now erected in his honour between him and his creation or his view that he had no other option but to respond.

The sacrifices that Cornelius had been giving became the power behind his words to the extent that God had to pay attention and answer the prayers of a heathen.

Watch this; the angel told Cornelius; you prayed then your giving came up before God to back up the words you spoke in prayer. It became a memorial.

A memorial is established to remind someone of an event or person, as long as it is there you can never be forgotten. Cornelius found a way to make his prayer a priority in the eyes of God. Even though he was not a Jew there was something else that stood behind the words he spoke in prayer that God deemed to be more valuable than even the prayers of some of the saints that were praying at that time. He could not ignore it.

It is valuable to know that the Greek word translated as memorial is *'mnemosynon'* which literally means *a record* or *memorandum*, also means *to rehearse*. It forced God to repeat what had happened, he rehearsed the matter. He was going over and over what Cornelius had presented. It became an echo. Every time God sat on his throne, what Cornelius had done echoed.

The memorial was like a huge wall that caused God not see his own angels, there was something blocking his view. He had to ask, **'who put up this wall and what does he want?'** He couldn't ignore it! The purpose of a memorial is also to remind people of a particular event or a person and normally people erect huge monuments as memorials. They are meant to be in your face, every time you walk past it you will be reminded what it's for. Even when you are home enjoying a cup of tea the moment you look out the window you cannot miss its towering figure from a distance. That thing keeps reminding you of the reason why it is there.

Now imagine God is in heaven and this thing is rising before him and he realizes that the man responsible for this is not a Jew but at the same time the thing that is now backing his prayer is way more valuable than what even the Jews are presenting, he had no option but to answer the prayer of a heathen.

It is like you having the preference of buying the house you are living in and renting, you already occupy the house and under United Kingdom of Great Britain law you should be given first preference if and when your Landlord decides to sell. The only difficulty then arises when you present as payment for the property your bearer's checks which have nothing to back them up as a currency. At the same time someone else who has just migrated to the United Kingdom of Great Britain puts in an offer in Pound sterling, the landlord has no choice but to weigh the value of your offer against the new bidder who has money backed by some real value.

No matter how much he likes you, he cannot ignore what the new bidder is proposing and when the hammer falls you will lose that property. God couldn't ignore this memorial that was now in front of him. I'm telling you if it was possible for angels to preach the gospel, then Cornelius would have been the first to receive Christ after hearing the sermon of an angel. But God had to send for Peter to come and preach to Cornelius and how grand he did it. He sent an angel.

Notice that the bible only says that Cornelius prayed but never actually tells us what his prayer request was, all we know is that the man was praying and giving. But in sending Peter for Cornelius to receive Christ, God answered every prayer request he could have ever had, because in Christ all things belong to us.

Romans 8: 32
He that spared not his own Son, but delivered him up for us all, how shall he not with him also freely give us all things?

By that one act Cornelius had secured eternal redemption for all Gentiles, that is how powerful the prayer of Cornelius was. When God commanded Peter to go to Cornelius he had just opened up all things that only the Jews had enjoyed up to this point. By receiving Christ there was now nothing else that could be kept from Cornelius, he just received the answer to every prayer he could ever say.

His giving had given value to his prayer. He had managed to present that thing that God told me he looks for in prayer, value.

Many in the body of Christ today will spend hours in prayer with very little or no results at all. The value behind prayer is not in how many hours you do, no! Not that you must not pray for long but understand why the long prayers you have been making go unanswered. You can pray for hours just enjoying the presence of God, fellowshipping with him and that is commendable. There is also this misconception that if you pray for long that prayer is powerful, you are wrong.

There is no value behind those prayers, it's like taking a tissue paper form your toilet and writing a dollar sign on it then go shopping, they will literally laugh at you before they arrest you and throw you in the mental asylum.

There is no value in the medium of exchange you are presenting. You can take tons and tons of those notes, if they have no value you are just piling up rubbish. So, it is not how many hours you do in prayer that makes your prayer to be effective. Remember the words you are speaking in prayer are just a **medium of exchange**, God is waiting to see the true value of what you are bringing.

Look at James 5: 17;

Elijah was a man subject to like passions as we are, and he prayed earnestly that it might not rain and it rained not on the earth by the space of three years and six months.

I know when the bible said earnest prayer there you thought it meant this was a very long prayer that Elijah was praying. Oh, no its pointing you to the power that was behind the words that Elijah was saying in prayer. Notice verse 16 calls it; "the effectual fervent prayer".

James 5: 16b
The effectual fervent prayer of a righteous man avails much.

The Greek word there for fervent is *energeo*, that word means energy. There is a spiritual energy behind the prayer. It's now more than just words that are being spoken; they are backed up by something else. And we are not talking about his voice projection here, you can shout all you like as long as there is nothing behind the words you are speaking you will have nothing to show for it.

You can just decide while you are sitting in your house, that now I am going to pray that God gives me a new car by the end of the week. Just because you put the dollar sign on it doesn't mean that people have to honour it. It's the same thing with you, just because you prayed doesn't mean there is value to your praying.

Imagine if I take a piece of toilet roll right now and write $2million and say to you here is $2million, you will never accept it. Why? Because you know its not currency and how do you know its not currency? Is it because of the artwork or the fact that it's a tissue paper? No, you won't accept it because it is not recognized as legal tender but then now we need to understand the reason why any money is accepted as legal tender.

It is because the reserve bank has approved it, it has some backing that it has. It may simply be the fact that there is demand people want it, but again why would anyone want it? People will only want it because of the backing that it has, it might be the fact that the economy of that country is going up. So, the reason why the currency of that nation is strong is because of the backing it has in the economy of that nation.

If there was no economy to talk about, it would just be as worthless as the scrap paper that a two year old has scribbled on in crayon. So believers are busy presenting before God a medium of exchange that has no backing, you are presenting worthless pieces of paper before him and demanding goods in exchange and you wonder why you are not receiving anything.

When God answered the prayer of Cornelius even the disciples of Jesus were confused, Peter who had received the instructions to go to Cornelius in a vision, even had to explain himself before they could accept this thing. It seemed as if God had broken his own rules in answering the prayer of Cornelius.

In John 9:31 we read;

"Now we know that God does not hear sinners; but if anyone is a worshiper of God and does His will, he hears him."

Notice first of all, that the Jews said, **"We know."** They did not say "We think" or "in our opinion." Now how did they "know" this? It had to come from God's word, it was not just something they thought up, they could prove it by scripture, they "knew" it so what they were saying here was a fact. Cornelius had managed to break the mould somehow.

Cornelius' prayer and generous heart drew a dramatic response from God. All the time he was giving he was building himself a memorial in Heaven until the point came when Cornelius had God's full attention and he responded to his needs. When Peter met Cornelius he reiterated what the angel had said, "Your prayer has been heard, and your alms are remembered in the sight of God." (Acts 10:31)

Look at the emphasis of Peter's words "...are remembered". They are present tense – a present and permanent reminder before God. It meant that God would continually be reminded of Cornelius' needs and then act on his behalf.

A woman with expensive ointment

In the Gospels we read of a woman who built herself a memorial through her actions. She had in her possession a very expensive jar of ointment. She may have received it via family inheritance or she may have been keeping it as an investment to provide for her old age. But whatever the reason, she was overcome with love for Jesus and her chief desire was to serve him, so she broke the jar and poured the fragrant ointment on him in an astonishing act of worship.

It is interesting to note that she was immediately criticized for her actions. It is amazing how people will often pour scorn upon sacrificial acts of worship to God. Lavish displays of worship and generous tokens of love offend the worldly-minded, but they provide sweet and fragrant worship to Jesus. Jesus defended the woman against her attackers.

Mark 14: 8- 9
She has done what she could. She has come beforehand to anoint My body for burial. Assuredly, I say to you, wherever this gospel is

preached throughout the whole world, what this woman did will also be spoken of as a memorial to her.

Jesus promised that this woman's sacrificial giving would be remembered, and it was. It was recorded in the Gospels for future generations to hear about. More importantly, this lady's offering was recorded and remembered in Heaven. She is now reaping her eternal reward. You might wonder how much would one have to give before God responded as dramatically as he did to these people? The woman's ointment was worth the equivalent of a whole year's salary, but that is not the point here. Jesus said of her, "She did what she could."

The scent of that perfume as expensive as it was is long gone now, but here we are, still talking about what she did. It became a memorial; to this day we are talking about it. There are many others that brought their gifts to the master during that time I can assure you, but their names are not even recorded in the bible.

An offering that you decide to make in order to honour God could cost you a year's salary, or it could be what you earn in one week – or anything the Holy Spirit lays on your heart. The amount is not the issue. Doing what we can to honour God and bless others is the point. The woman did what "she could" meaning the best of her ability not the best of her stinginess!

When it comes to giving, listen carefully to the Holy Spirit and allow him to speak to you about you requests. He will show you when and how, and how much to give and God will bless you not because you gave a gift, but through your attitude of heart's response to his grace.

The Lord Jesus pointed us to the ability of a sacrifice to build a memorial yet believers are still praying empty prayers and as we go into this next chapter I am ripping the whole thing open, flip the page at your own risk I'm taking no prisoners!

Chapter 3

The Prayer of an Unbeliever

'The prayers of my people are no different to the prayers of a drunkard who has never seen a church pew in his life, I am under no obligation to answer such prayers. They are praying like heathens and hypocrites. It is only out of my own mercy and grace that I intervene.'

Just by that one statement, I knew what I was about to learn would redefine my concept of prayer, hold on to your seat again because this chapter will mess up your theology completely.

Most people spend hours in all night prayer meetings, they actually think that the length of their prayers or the time they pray will give them value, this is far from the truth. This is the very same problem that the Lord Jesus was addressing in the book of Matthew, watch this;

Matthew 6: 7
But when ye pray, use not vein repetitions, as the heathen do: for they think that they shall be heard for their much speaking.

I thought I knew where the Lord was going with this when He quoted that scripture, I didn't know that I was about to get the shock of my life.

Notice something here, the bible is actually telling us there is a way that heathens pray, remember the scripture is saying that;

'don't pray as the heathens do'.

He was pointing out to his disciples the fact that the way they were praying at this point in time, was no different to the way sinners were praying.

So unbelievers are out there praying, just as much as you do, nevertheless in vain, but they have a certain way of doing it, and the Lord is now instructing his disciples to not pray in the same manner as those that are not saved.

Statistically, one in two unbelievers pray daily, just in case!

An Evil Prayer

So you can be praying but your prayer to God appear in the same way as the prayer of the heathen, yet you are speaking in tongues, quoting the **'thee's and thou's'** of the King James version of the bible. Yet God looks at it like the prayer of a heathen, an unbeliever who has never confessed Christ. It's like Osama Bin Laden praying to God and expecting a miracle.

You can imagine, the angels in heaven are not in hurry to come to your assistance and God does not pay attention to that kind of prayer. This is the same thing the bible tells us in the book of James;

James 4: 3
Ye ask and receive not, because you ask amiss, that you may consume it upon your own pleasures.

Notice, even God knows that you have been praying and that it's not working, the bible says; '*ye ask and receive not,*' He acknowledges the fact that you have been asking, but just tells you it is not working. Think about it, God himself knows that there are prayers you are saying right now, that will never be answered and he says it right there. But right there he points to the same problem in Matthew 6, watch this, the bible says;

'ye pray amiss'.

This is where the English version of the bible does us a great injustice you see, when the bible says that you pray amiss. The Greek word translated as amiss is *'kakos'* and it means evil, bad physically or morally, diseased or sick. God was literally calling that type of prayer an evil prayer. Think about it, this is you, on your knees praying for hours and God looks at it and says as for this prayer, it's an evil thing. It is a sick prayer. You are praying like a heathen, an unbeliever.

Don't get me wrong here; it is not the words you utter in prayer that are evil, no! It is the way the prayer is being done, you are praying amiss, the way you are doing it is the evil part not the words being spoken.

Like many, you might be thinking, but I never blaspheme when I pray, I only ask for God to protect me or bless me. However, you are deviating from the prescribed order of prayer. You are praying **KAKOS**. You are praying an EVIL PRAYER. You prayer is sick. You are praying AMISS!

It is not in the words that are said in prayer but in the fact that you have deviated from the prescribed way of doing it, you are now praying amiss. When you do that your prayer becomes evil, anything that you take and deviate from the original form is what the bible calls wicked. That means that you had something that was good in its original form but you have twisted and turned it from the original even though God created it to begin with, that thing is now wicked. It is now perverted.

Let me show you something amazing. Understand that the word SIN is derived from archery where an archer shoots an arrow from a bow and in an attempt to hit the bullseye, misses it. That is called SIN in archery meaning 'missing the mark', so prayer like this becomes a SIN because it has missed the mark. It is **KAKOS**!

The devil himself is called the wicked one that's because the way that he is now, is not the same way that God created him. He missed the mark!

Ezekiel 28: 15
Thou was perfect in thy ways from the day that thou wast created, till iniquity was found in thee.

Even Satan was perfect when he was created by God, flawless in everything that he was doing. He would minister in the very presence of a God who cannot tolerate sin, yet he managed to turn even that which was pure to become the greatest evil. It became wicked, it was twisted from its original form.

It's the same thing believers are doing in prayer, to the extent that when you now pray, your prayer appears in the same way as the prayers of those that are evil and don't even serve God. You are deviating from the prescribed way of doing it and actually making the whole thing wicked. You are praying '*kakos*'. You are praying amiss.

You are about to get the shock of your life right now so let us go back to the book of Matthew and see exactly what the Lord Jesus was teaching.

Matthew 6: 3- 5
But when thou doest alms, let not thy left hand know what thy right hand doeth: That thine alms may be in secret and thy Father which seeth in

secret himself shall reward thee openly. And when thou prayest, thou shalt not be as the hypocrites are: for they love to pray standing in the synagogues and in the corners of the streets, that they may be seen of men.

Don't lose me here, if you read from the very beginning of chapter 6 of the book of Matthew, Jesus is instructing his disciples on how to **give right,** up to verse 5 when he says;

'**and when you pray**'.

The biggest problem here is that many fail to see the connection between the instruction to give and the prayer.

You need to realize that the bible was not written in verses and chapters, that is why verse 5 begins with word '**and**' it is connected to the previous verse. What he is teaching in verse 5 is the same thing he was talking about from the very beginning of the chapter.

But there is something I don't want you to miss right there, watch this. The word translated as '**and**' as I mentioned before is the Greek word *kahee* which means then or therefore. In other words, we could read it this way;

" that thine alms may be in secret: and thy father which seeth in secret himself shall reward thee

*openly And (**then, therefore, kahee**) when you pray, thou shalt **not** be as the hypocrites are,".*

Are you getting this? Jesus was not just expecting and instructing the disciples to give in the right way, oh no! He was telling then how to give in order to reveal the prescribed way to pray.

Look at it, the point to the whole teaching was not giving at all, it was prayer!

He knew there was no way they could ever pray right until they caught the first part if this praying business was going to do them any good. When you read further down you will find that this is the same chapter that the Lord taught his disciples what many refer to as 'the Lord's prayer'.

In fact, that particular prayer is mentioned twice in the gospels it is also found in the book of Luke, and Luke felt it important for us to know the reason why the Lord was actually teaching them how to pray.

Luke 11:1
And it came to pass, that, as he was praying in a certain place, when he ceased, one of his disciples said unto him, Lord, teach us to pray, as John also taught his disciples.

You see, up to this point the Lord had not taught them how to pray, but the disciples of John were praying. Think about it, the Lord Jesus had to be prompted by his own disciples to teach them how to pray. Until this time he didn't think it was necessary?

Don't lose me here, the disciples of Jesus and the disciples of John both had needs that should have been presented in prayer. But it is only the disciples of John that were praying, how then were the disciples of Jesus getting their needs met without saying a single prayer?

It seems as if they were getting by just fine without praying at all, it wasn't even their needs that pushed them to want to pray.

That is because even though they had not yet learnt the how to articulate their prayers the substance that makes the prayer valuable was already speaking on their behalf. They were not lacking anything because they were already receiving the answers to their prayer even though they were not praying.

I am not saying that you should stop praying all together but you need to settle in your heart what God really sees in your prayer. I know this is difficult for the religious mind to grasp, but remember **God does not answer prayer**, but acts in response to the thing that gives prayer value. As long as the basis of prayer was going up before the Lord they were receiving answers to prayers they never prayed.

The prayer you say at night before you go to bed is only a **medium of exchange**, God looks for what backs the currency or medium of exchange that you have just presented.

At this point in time even the disciples didn't understand why they didn't lack anything that the disciples of John had, even though they were not praying. It is only when they observed the ritual application of prayer being practiced by the disciples of John that they also thought, yeah we need to pray.

This is the reason why the Lord Jesus was quick to point out to them not be like the hypocrites who love to be seen praying in the streets and synagogues that they may have glory of men. He was addressing their motive for wanting to pray because it wasn't out of need that they wanted to pray, they were already sufficiently supplied.

The inflation of prayer

Now before we go any further I really want us to dig deeper into what the Lord was teaching here in the book of Matthew. Watch this; lets read from verse 3;

Matthew 6: 3- 4
But when thou doest alms, let not thy left hand know what thy right hand doeth: That thine alms may be in secret: and thy Father which seeth in secret himself shall reward thee openly.

The Lord's instruction here seems rather confusing because if you think about it, in that day and age what they used to present as offerings and alms would have been in the form of livestock or grain. How then do you put your goat on the alter with your right hand without your left hand knowing about it? It doesn't make any sense because it's a figure of speech. What he meant was that what you give is not meant to be the thing that gains you recognition from the people you are giving or those who see you doing it.

Many believers make this mistake, the day they give their biggest offering they want the man of God to know about it, in fact they want the whole church to know that they are the ones that paid for the PA system, or the new cameras in church.

You have just missed it right there you are now creating your memorial in front of people that don't have the ability to answer your prayer. Your gift and your alms are meant to appear before God in the same way that Cornelius did, but it never happens no matter how much you give because you enjoy the recognition you get from those who are down here.

Your gift fails to become a memorial before God because you have just used the building blocks for men to see how good you are or what a wonderful thing you have done. The bible says; **'they have their reward'**, by the time you say your prayer it no longer has anything to back it, because you have just spent it right here on earth.

Matthew 6: 2 says;

Therefore when thou doest thine alms, do not sound a trumpet before thee, as the hypocrites do in the synagogues and in the streets, that they may have glory of men. Verily I say unto you, They have their reward.

You are now presenting to God a medium of exchange that has no value at all its already spent. This is why you will hear people say; *'I give but it never seems to work for me'.* They are devaluing their medium of exchange, their prayers without even knowing it.

But look at the very next verse;

Matthew 6: 4
That thine alms may be in secret and thy Father which seeth in himself shall reward thee openly.

It is only when your giving is not done to impress the masses out there that it can appear before the Lord. Look at it', the bible is telling us that the Father sees the thing that is done in secret. In other words the thing you do openly to get glory from men he does not see at all. It becomes **KAKOS**. It becomes a fake currency. It fails to become a memorial before God, I can assure you that there are many that were giving during the days of Cornelius but they never built a memorial before God.

The MOTIVE Test

Have you ever given sacrificially and after giving, the pastor thanks everyone else for their service and forgets to mention your name? You leave that place offended, fuming about how ungrateful people are, by that one act you have just withdrawn your gift from the secret place, you have taken it out of the view of God. You now building a statue, a memorial before many people and removing the thing that was going to arrest God's attention!

Remember the Lord Jesus said;

"the Father sees in secret"

So, when you parade what you have done before men it ceases to exist in the secret place where God can see it. By the time your knees hit the floor for you to pray you are now just speaking empty words they have no value at all. Remember it is not the words you speak when you are praying that guarantee the answer to your prayer.

Psalm 91: 1 says;
He that dwelleth in the secret place of the most High shall abide under the shadow of the Almighty.

Now when we talk about the secret place we are not talking about some hidden place in your house or in the bush. Here we are talking about the very presence of God and that is exactly where the alms and prayers of Cornelius were found. So you can give but then your seed and prayer fail to get into the secret place, the presence of God where he can see it. It is as if you have not done anything at all, there is nothing registered in heaven on your account.

There is nothing to back your prayer, there is no value to it at all and to God even though you are in church every Sunday and wear a cross round your neck every day this is the prayer of a sinner.

I need you to follow very closely as we go into this next chapter as I delve deeper into the scriptures I strongly advise that you sit down wherever you are, this will go down with a kick hang on.

Chapter 4

The Day God chose Satan over his people

"Do you realize that there is a day I turned against my own people and sided with their enemy just because I could not ignore the value that backed their enemy's prayer. I turned against Israel and they lost the battle to a heathen king".

My mind was racing and I couldn't think of a single scripture where God took the devil's side against his people but before I could voice my objection came the answer to my question;

"look at 2 Kings 3". He said.

2 Kings 3: 27
Then he took his eldest son that should have reigned in his stead, and offered him for a burnt offering upon the wall. And there was great indignation against Israel and they departed from him, and returned to their own land.

The king of Moab had just taken his eldest son and sacrificed him as a burnt offering while the battle was raging, they were heading for certain defeat. I want you to consider this carefully. I know human sacrifices were a common thing in those days, but this wasn't just one of the king's slaves that had been placed on the alter here. This was his only son!

This particular boy was the heir to his throne, apart from being his own blood, he had invested years in preparing him to take over his kingdom. This is the only son who would have been allowed into the king's court to learn from the wisest advisors of the king. Years of mentorship had been invested in that boy. He was set to take over from his father. This boy was the prince.

This was not a son that he could replace just like that, he would have been 'the adopted son' among all the king's sons. That means he is the one of however many sons the king had, that had been tested and deem to be fit to become the next king. In those days you just did not become the heir to your father's throne just because you are the eldest, you also needed to prove your worth among the other sons before you could be endorsed as the next in line to the throne.

You see, many times the bible when it says the 'only son' or 'eldest son' it also means the one meant to take over or the mature one, meaning there could have been many sons but only one tested and worthy to be the king in his stead. This had nothing to do with age. This boy was the mature one and suitable to take over!

Now you can understand how deep a sacrifice this was. Just short of his own life the king had sacrificed the greatest possession he had, the very future of his kingdom.

Now notice, until this point the Israelites had been winning the battle according to the word of the prophet Elisha.

I know what you are thinking right now; 'but God hates evil how can he take sides with the enemy?' I couldn't get my mind around it, it is one thing for God to answer the prayers of Cornelius but it's a whole different ball game when God turns on his own people in favour of one who is fighting his own people.

Think about this, the Lord God almighty standing with his own people and in the middle of the battle that they are winning and decides I'm switching sides, there is something that the enemy has done which my people have failed to do.

Watch what **Luke 16: 8** says.

...the children of this world are in their generation wiser than the children of light.

This is why I said the children of darkness are wiser in the generation than the children of light (Luke 16: 8).

If you notice that every one that goes into the occult or black magic will never perform any ritual without a sacrifice. Right now if you do the research you will find that anyone who has ever consulted a witch doctor will tell you that even before they state their business, the first thing they do is that they present their offering. Every witch doctor knows to never bother preforming any ritual without a sacrifice, they know it's a waste of time because they understand the law of the spiritual realm. That law says nothing spiritual can be released without the natural.

No wonder even in the days of Elijah the mantle had to come off for the double portion to follow.

The children of darkness now know that they cannot just utter their enchantments without an offering or a sacrifice behind it. They know that the power is not in the mere words that they speak, but in the sacrifice that gives their words substance. They also know the power is not in the witch doctor unlike Christians who think the power is in their man or woman of God.

Their words and enchantments are a mere **medium of exchange** in the realm of the spirit, the thing that is actually considered is what backs those words. They have understood how to be heard in the realm of the spirit and yet the church still has no idea what makes a prayer valuable.

Empty words

This is exactly why you can take the same prayer another saint prayed and got an answer, you will recite the same prayer word for word to no avail. God is not just answering the words you are saying in prayer. This why the Lord said; "that he does not answer prayer, but that the prayer is a mere **medium of exchange** that requires something to back it."

Prayer is more than just a play of words, otherwise we would just write book upon book of all the prayers that God has answered for you to parrot back to him and receive the same thing.

Now I want you to really look at this thing. The world has caught the revelation and the church is still doing the same thing and expecting a different result, that's madness. Someone still thinks, yes I prayed I should receive a miracle now yet all you have done is present a medium of exchange that has no value whatsoever. You are speaking empty words.

Even though the Moabite King was not serving the Lord neither was his sacrifice for him in the realm of the spirit it appeared as something monumental. Bigger than anything the camp of Israel who had been promised victory even attempted, to the extent that God looked at it and felt cheated by his own people. It seems as if the enemy who had no power to deliver the Moabites, received more honor than the God of the universe was receiving from his own people.

You also need to understand that the Israelites had received a prophetic word to win this battle by God himself and we know God doesn't lie but here he switched sides and reversed his own promise based on the value of a sacrifice that was given by the enemy of his own people. That shows his prophetic word was cemented only by a value that was beyond their cries and failure to present that value meant the word was also not set in stone.

There was a price tag attached to that sacrifice, it cost him something, his heart was in it. It became a righteous prayer although he himself was KAKOS. It arrested God's attention and made God to be disturbed in heaven so to speak. Hope you are catching this revelation?

The robbery of prayer

God in his frustration allowed the Israelites to suffer defeat at the hands of the enemy he had promised they would conquer. In the realm of the spirit it was as if the Israelites had offered a ton of wheat as an offering to the Lord and the enemy wheeled in ten tons of Gold to give to a false God.

The two were incomparable!

Have you ever brought an average school term report card, which your parents were kind of 'ok' with, that is until your sister walks in with straight A's. All of a sudden the 'C' on your report card no longer goes down well with the old man. What happened? Your sister's report card just shed a bit more light on yours and changed the scale by which it was being measured.

All of a sudden they realize how much better you could have done, this is exactly were the children of Israel found themselves. The enemy's sacrifice had exposed their own ingratitude to God and he turned on them like an enemy. The medium of exchange that was behind the enemy was far greater than what the Israelites were prepared to do, yet the two wanted the same thing, victory in battle. God looked at it and said; they have robbed me.

Lets look at this carefully, if you were selling a car today and I came and offered you a thousand dollars for it and just before we filled in the paperwork to transfer ownership, somebody else comes in and offered you ten thousand dollars for the same vehicle. All of a sudden you realize that you had literally given it away. There is no way you would give me that car for a thousand dollars when somebody else wants it for ten times more. If anything you may even be offended that I had offered you so little for it to begin with.

Again, I am not saying that the human sacrifice was pleasing to God, but that in the realm of the spirit it became a far greater monument than what the Israelites had offered even though it didn't appeal to God. There was something greater backing up the medium of exchange that the enemy was using, his currency in the spirit was more valuable. God then looked at what his own people had done, and changed his mind about giving them victory.

The Moabite king's sacrifice did not have the power to defeat the Israelis, it was God himself who decided to turn the tables around when he realized that the enemy actually had a better understanding than his own people.

It was really daylight robbery. This is exactly why king David made this statement in second Samuel.

2 Samuel 24: 24
And the king said to Araunah, Nay; but I will surely buy it of thee at a price: neither will I offer burnt offerings unto the Lord my God of that which doth cost me nothing.

David understood the importance of placing value into the medium of exchange that you are presenting to God. If something doesn't cost you anything that means it has very little value according to you, what more when you take it to God? It becomes worthless, many are stuck right now and wonder why their prayers never seem to produce any results.

Increasing the value of prayer

David was saying that even though he could receive all the things for free, he could not take it to God and present it as something valuable when it cost him nothing. There is no sacrifice in something that costs you nothing.

Look at **Mark 12: 41 - 43** and see what Jesus said;

As Jesus was sitting opposite the treasury, He watched the crowd placing money into it. And many rich people put in large amounts. Then one poor widow came and put in two small copper coins, which amounted to a small fraction of a denarius. Jesus called His disciples to Him and said, "Truly I tell you, this poor widow has put more than all the others into the treasury....

Notice something here, according to the Lord the old lady who put in two copper coins had given more than all the others, yet we are told that the amount she had given was far less than the others. How then does God place more value in the little than in what was seemingly a greater offering according to your own understanding?

This is where many people miss it right here, it is not what you give that determines the value behind the prayer but what you are left with after you have given. What did it cost you to give what you have just given? That old lady had given all she had, it was not a lot but it was a 100 percent all she was worth. The rest had given more out of their abundance and what they gave was nowhere near what this old lady had in putting value behind her medium of exchange.

Look at it again the bible actually tells us that;

'many that were rich cast in much'.

But still in the eyes of the Lord what they gave was nowhere near what this poor old lady had done. Whenever you talk about sacrifice many believers are quick to hide behind their needs or lack. They want to be excused and in their minds they justify their own stinginess thinking that God should understand.

It doesn't work that way, during one of my live broadcast there was a young man in South Africa who had lost his scholarship that he needed to carry on with his education. He had been praying for a miracle to no avail and that day he decided he was going to give. All he had in his account was $1.50, he didn't know where he was going to get the fees for the next semester or where his next meal was going to come from.

That day he took his seed of a $1.50 and gave it to the Lord, I know to many it doesn't sound like a lot, but this is all he had. He had given 100 percent. The very next day he received an email notifying him that his scholarship had just been restored. He managed to put value behind his prayer because of his sacrifice. It was only a $1.50 seed. That's hardly enough to change the world but it spoke volumes, this was all he had.

You need to catch this; it is not necessarily the amount that you have given that determines the value behind your words in prayer but how much you are left with after you give. What I'm about to share with you in this next chapter challenged and turned my theology on its head, pay close attention.

Chapter 5

Counterfeit Prayer

"Most believers are swindlers they are bringing to me counterfeit prayers. My anger was kindled against Ananias and Sapphira when they tried to bring to me a counterfeit prayer. It was an evil prayer. To me it was as if the devil himself was doing their bidding."

Immediately I had a big problem with this statement, I never knew of any scripture where Ananias had made a prayer request, yet the Lord was now telling me that the reason he punished them was that their prayer was fake. It was counterfeit. How could this be?

"You have already forgotten what I told you in the beginning, I do not answer prayer, I have never answered prayer, it is only a medium of exchange I only respond to what backs prayer."

Just like you I was still caught up in what we actually say in prayer but what I heard next blew me right out of the water. The Lord pointed me to the book of Ephesians.

Ephesians 3: 20
Now unto him that is able to do exceeding abundantly above all that we ask or think, according to the power that worketh in us.

I want you to look at this carefully. Why would God boast in his ability to provide for us beyond what we ask or even think when he has no intention of doing it? In this scripture he was actually pointing us to the fact that his provision goes beyond what we ask or think. But wait a minute, when do we ask? In prayer of course! So then he is literally telling us that he is able to do more than what we can utter in prayer.

This scripture would be meaningless if God couldn't or wouldn't provide for us anything that has not been said in prayer. This is because when God answers prayer he is not limited by the words you speak in prayer, remember your prayer is only a **medium of exchange** what he is really responding to is what backs your prayer.

Voice of unspoken prayer

Like I said in the previous chapters, if what God is answering is the thing behind your prayer then it becomes possible for God to answer your prayer before you even speak a word because the backing for your prayer has already presented itself to the Lord. God is now acting in response to what backs your prayer before you present the medium of exchange. This is why he can answer before you pray;

Look at **Isaiah 65: 24** again.
Before they call I will answer, while they are yet speaking I will answer.

He answers before they call because he is not answering their call, but the thing that backs that call. So he no longer needs to wait for them to call for him to answer, once he sees the backing for their prayer that's sufficient to warrant an answer from God. Remember the words you are saying in prayer are just a **medium of exchange.** They are a mere representation, they are the means by which you bring what you are exchanging. They are standing in place of the real thing of value that God looks at when he answers prayer.

Back to Ananias

To further understand Ananias and Safira sin you have to understand another line of revelation. Way back money was in silver coins and gold coins that carried a certain weight. However there existed thieves in those days that would shave off some of the silver or gold from the coins and create more coins but they left the other coins with less value than what was written on them. This is the same with Ananias and Safira. They presented a shaved off value. It missed the mark. It became **KAKOS**.

They went for the value that was less than what they had promised God. When Ananias went to present his gift to the apostles, to God it went up as a *kakos* prayer, there were no words that had been spoken but the foundation of prayer had already been laid. To God this was an evil thing that was coming up before him. Ananias tried to bring in a currency that was shaved off. It had the real qualities but still counterfeit. The value written on it did not correspond with its value making it counterfeit.

Its like you taking a twenty dollar note and penciling in another zero so it reads two hundred when you know that the value of the note you are presenting is only twenty dollars. You would be prosecuted if you tried to deposit that note in your bank account, why? It's a counterfeit although it's the real paper with approved watermark and all but that zero you added to the twenty makes it fake. That is exactly what Ananias had done. He had taken something that was good and twisted it into something evil before God.

Acts 5: 3 says;

But Peter said, Ananias, why hath Satan filled thine heart to lie to the Holy Ghost, and to keep back part of the price of the land?

For you to understand that this was a *kakos* or evil prayer before God, Peter actually points us to the origin of this evil act when he asks the question;

"why hath Satan filled your heart?"

To God this very act was demonic, it was a *kakos* and there was no other prayer that could now be made for Ananias, even Peter couldn't help.

This is exactly how the devil operates, he misrepresents what he has in order to entice you. When God looked at what Ananias had done, he could see the devil's footprints all over it. It was demonic. Ananias had just messed up the very foundation of prayer anything else he was going to say from that point would be stained.

It's the same thing as you having a currency backed by gold only to discover that the gold in your bullion is actually iron ore, it doesn't matter from that point what kind of design you put on the notes for your currency, its worth is determined by what backs it. It becomes criminal for you to misrepresent what you actually have, it makes you a fraud. That's the same situation Ananias found himself.

Ananias had actually determined in his heart that he was going to deceive God, he knew exactly what he had sold the piece of land for, but when the question came he decided to answer untruthfully. Many today are doing the exact same thing as Ananias and are surprised when their prayers go unanswered.

The biggest problem Ananias had is that he messed up the very thing that gives voice to your prayer and after that he didn't have a leg to stand on.

When the time to give comes, many believers today already know what they want in their hearts and when they come before the Lord with their offering or sacrifice just like Ananias they are quickly moved by the enemy from their original intentions. You really know that I should give two hundred dollars today, but before you do it the 'kind' voice of the devil begins to speak to you.

Now all of a sudden you remember your car is due for a service at the end of the month or you need to get a burger on your way home and before you know it you are only giving a quarter of what God had laid on your heart to do. You have just fallen into the same trap as Ananias, you have just allowed the enemy to fill your heart with deceit. But you tell yourself its ok God understands.

You are now doubting even God's ability to provide before you even sow. This is exactly why the bible says;

"a double minded man cannot receive anything from the Lord he is unstable in all his ways".

His inability to act immediately when God speaks will always rob him of the blessing he desires.

What the Lord taught me on prayer exposed the scandal in the church today, as believers are robbing their Lord. I know, I just said it, let us go into this next chapter you will find out exactly what I mean and it will help you master **The Prayer That God Can't Ignore**.

Chapter 6

Robbing God

Ananias had attempted to swindle the Lord, but before you judge him let me point out that he is not the only one, some of you as you read will find yourself entangled in this same controversy. You may also be a swindler trying to con God.

Malachi 3: 8

Will a man rob God? Yet ye have robbed me. But ye say, wherein have we robbed thee? In tithes and offerings.

But how could anybody rob God of anything? Does it mean that we storm the ramparts of heaven and break into the inner sanctum of the divine treasury and help ourselves to things that God alone possesses? Such a thing is physically impossible. The strongest robber in the world could never scale the heights of heaven and plunder the possessions of an omnipotent God, and so the very idea of robbing God seems crazy.

Yet God gives answer to this question immediately dispelling any absurdity connected with it. He explains pointedly how indeed it is possible for his own children to be guilty of robbery against God. He answers this question, "Will man rob God?"

saying, "Yet you are robbing me." The Israelite response is:

"How have we robbed you?" To which God replies, "In your tithes and offerings" Malachi 3:8

The Israelites were now bringing as their tithe the weakest of their flock, the lame and maimed is what they would bring to God as their tithes and offering. The tithe in those days was meant to be a tenth of the very best of their crops and flock yet they were now defrauding God.

In the same way that your sacrifice is able to build a memorial before the Lord, the tithes and offerings are meant to enforce the blessing that God has placed on every believer. Don't get me wrong here, I am not saying that your tithes and offerings will build the memorial for your prayer, no! They have nothing to do with your prayer request, just your standing and the blessing that is appointed for every child of God.

But even in tithes and offerings the Israelites had robbed God, back in those days they didn't have credit cards and the paper notes that we use as medium of exchange today. The earliest form of money they came up with was gold and silver coins. Even Judas betrayed the Lord for 30 pieces of silver, but even those coins were not fool proof. People had already devised ways of cheating and misrepresenting what they actually had.

Like I said before they would take the silver or gold coins and shave off a bit of the edges of the coin and just leave enough for you to believe that they were the same size as the originals. This is why they introduced scales so they could weigh in the silver and gold to make sure it represented the value that the individual was demanding.

This cancer had also crept into the church and in Malachi God is exposing their deceit when he says,

'you have robbed me'.

The Israelites knew that is was possible to pay someone and rob them at the same time.

They had actually alienated themselves from God and their prayer life was now suffering. This was the priesthood of Israel that God was speaking to in Malachi but makes a shocking revelation in verse 7 of Malachi 3 watch this;

Even from the days of your fathers ye are gone away from mine ordinances, and have not kept them. Return unto me, and I will return unto you, saith the Lord of hosts. But ye said, wherein shall we return?

At this point in time the Israelites were still carrying out all the ceremonial rituals that were commanded in the Law of Moses and yet God is saying they have departed from him. Right now, you are in church every Sunday you have never missed a communion service for a whole year yet your prayers are not entertained in the presence of God, you don't even have that kind of access.

Their deception had moved them from the secret place of the Most High and left them vulnerable. Notice, the Lord says;

"return unto me,"

That means they actually packed up and left the place of fellowship with God. But because they were still in church singing the hymns and shouting hallelujah this statement confused them and they asked,

"wherein shall we return?".

God did not mince his words in replying them;

"will a man rob God? Yet ye have robbed me."

Tithes and offerings were a foundational thing, notice they couldn't pray or fast to return to God, they could only come back the same way they left, through tithes and offerings.

They were now using diseased and maimed animals as their tithes and offerings, we know already from previous chapters that this is unacceptable to God, remember;

James 4: 3
Ye ask and receive not, because you ask amiss, that you may consume it upon your own pleasures.

The Greek word translated as **amiss** is *'kakos'* and it means evil, bad physically or morally, diseased or sick. And that is exactly what the Israelites were now bringing to God as tithes and offerings. God was literally calling that type of prayer an evil prayer because to God it was the same thing as bringing something that is diseased, sick or maimed before him. And that is exactly why God said you have robbed me.

The Israelites in those days like many of you today were surprised that God even notices those things.

Power of an 'unprayed' prayer

Now I want you to look again at the Lord's instructions in the book of Malachi Chapter 3 I know we have gone through the scripture already but what the Lord showed me I had never seen before. I need your undivided attention at this point.

Malachi 3: 10
Bring ye all the tithes into the storehouse, that there may be meat in mine house, and prove me now herewith, saith the Lord of hosts, if I will not

open you the windows of heaven, and pour you out a blessing, that there shall not be room enough to receive it.

At this point in time though they were God's own people, the Israelites were not enjoying the blessing of God. Like many believers today somehow they found themselves alienated from what should have been their heritage.

Right now if I ask you, you will be able to quote and list all the promises and blessings that are promised to every believer. However when we bring it down to which of those blessings you are actually enjoying as a believer that list becomes smaller and smaller. In the book of Malachi God answered for us that most difficult question.

Malachi 3: 11

And I will rebuke the devourer for your sakes, and he shall not destroy the fruits of your ground; neither shall your vine cast her fruit before the time in the field, saith the Lord of hosts.

There was definitely a problem here and the Israelites needed the intervention of God. For the Lord to even say that;

"I will rebuke the devourer for your sake"

It means they were in trouble. There was already a devourer on the scene, ransacking everything they had. Their crops were failing in the fields and there was an enemy behind it all.

I want you to notice even the language that God uses when it comes to things that affect a believer's finances, it seems as if he pulls out the big guns for that one. He actually refers to Himself as:

'the Lord of hosts"

Now I don't want you to lose me here. The Hebrew word translated as hosts is *tsaba* it literally means an army, a mass of persons regularly organized for war. He was literally telling them that I am the God of angel armies and I can put the enemy to flight on your behalf.

It just was not a matter of telling the plants to grow and be fruitful, no! There was an enemy behind their failures and when God addresses their situation he is also showing them his ability to conquer. We can actually read Malachi 3: 11 this way;

And I will rebuke the devourer for your sakes, and he shall not destroy the fruits of your ground; neither shall your vine cast her fruit before the time in the field, saith the Lord of angel armies.

There was a battle for their prosperity and they were crying out to God for a solution, but surprisingly he didn't ask them to go on a seven day fast. They were already asking God to prosper them but the words they were speaking in prayer were just not enough. There was nothing behind them, as **medium of exchange** it wasn't worth much.

It doesn't matter what else they were going to try and do, things were not going to change until they presented their tithes and offerings to God.

There are certain financial prayers that you are praying right now that will always go unanswered because you have not followed the prescribed way to prayer and have forsaken even the foundational truths of tithe and offering. You can cry out until you get blue in the face it will not happen for you.

When it comes to the financial prayer you always need a greater **medium of exchange** behind it, remember prayer is not merely in the words you utter in your prayer closet. Your words are only a medium of exchange. So then if there are now certain needs in your life to which God says when it comes to these I don't need to hear your prayer all I want to see is what backs your prayer. It only serves to confirm that we have something more powerful than the words we speak in prayer that we have not even taken advantage of.

All that Christians know to do is to cry out in their prayer closets, yet there is a time that you need the God of angel armies to intervene on your behalf. At that point there is only one thing that will speak for you and it is your giving that accompanies your prayer. That is what we call **THE PRAYER THAT GOD CANT IGNORE!**

Accelerated Prayer

If there are certain prayers that cannot be answered before you bring your seed or sacrifice that means your seed or sacrifice is higher than your prayer.

I will repeat that just in case you missed it. If you went into the shop to buy a pair of shoes and you presented a ten-dollar note and they say to you for this particular pair of shoes you need a twenty-dollar note. That means the twenty-dollar note is more valuable than the ten-dollar note. It doesn't take a rocket scientist to understand the sense in that.

So there are things you can buy with a twenty-dollar note that you cannot buy with a ten-dollar note. I know this next statement will confuse a good number of religious minds, just stay with me we are going somewhere. Everything you can buy with a ten-dollar note you can buy with twenty, I know you missed it right there.

If your seed or sacrifice can get a response where your prayer has failed that makes it more powerful than your prayer. It can achieve more. If your tithe and offering can open the windows of heaven where your prayer alone has failed that means your giving is more powerful than the prayer you have been saying.

Now watch this;

2 Corinthians 9: 10
Now he that ministereth seed to the sower both minister bread for your food, and multiply your seed sown, and increase the fruit of your righteousness.

So now the seed sown is no longer just speaking for your financial need, but Paul says that when you give God will,

"increase the fruit of your righteousness".

Remember the words you are speaking in prayer, are just the medium of exchange, God answers in response to what backs your prayer.

Because your seed or sacrifice has the ability to go beyond the words you say in prayer, it becomes easy for it to achieve those things that you used to achieve by prayer alone. The fruit of Righteousness should never be connected to a financial seed but we find it right there.

Righteousness itself is a gift we receive when we are saved, but when you sow your seed God says I will multiply the benefits of you having that gift of righteousness. Your seed or your offering represents the things that are most valuable to you. Think about it, you spent eight hours of your day at work.

A third of your life is spent working for money so there is no better thing that you can use to validate the things that are most important to you. The Moabite king in the previous chapter we read had sacrificed his own son. It spoke volumes because of all his treasures, his first born son was the closest to his heart. His sacrifice cost him something, it was valuable to him personally.

Matthew 6: 21 says;

For where your treasure is, there your heart will be also.

When you pray and quote scriptures you have presented your medium of exchange but when you give, your heart is now in it, there is now a backing to your words. There are no longer just empty words you are speaking just hoping to move God.

Acts 9: 36 concurs;

Now there was at Joppa a certain disciple named Tabitha, which by interpretation is called

Dorcas; this woman was full of good works alms deeds which she did.

Dorcas was a giver to such an extent that when she fell sick and died the people around her, the widows she used to look after, took some of the things she made and took them to Peter, pleading for her life. They understood that they could demand a resurrection from a financial seed. The weight of what Dorcas used to give went behind their cries and secured the answer they needed. Without it their cries would have just been another medium of exchange that has no backing at all.

Dorcas was not a one-time giver she had made a lifestyle of taking care of those in need. The reason why she could afford to give and keep giving, is because her seed was producing a financial harvest, but beyond that it was the same thing that brought her back from the dead.

Right now you are thinking, "if I just sacrifice I'm done, God has to respond". I was exactly like you until God opened my eyes to what I'm about to share with you in these last two chapters.

Chapter 7

The 419 Sacrifice

Believers are now so skilled in the art of deception when it comes to what they want from God. They have developed what I call the "419 Sacrifice" after the Nigerian 419 scam which has left many out of pocket around the world. The Nigerian 419 Scam comes in all shapes and sizes but the general gist of it is where you are told;

"...Just give us a $100 fee to process the $30million prize you have won in an online lottery"

Or;

"You are the sole beneficiary of an inheritance from your long lost uncle, send us a fee for processing".

You never get to see the prize or inheritance or the money you sent as processing fees. You have just been hoodwinked. You might say I won't fall for that 419, but you would be a fool to think so for many have fallen victims to this.

Many dream of winning the lottery one day, thinking that all their trouble will vanish, to the extent that when the scam presents itself they fall for it because they are so desperate to believe it.

419 Presents

Have you ever heard of husbands who buy their wives a cooker or refrigerator as a birthday present? When they bring it home they are expecting to sweep her off her feet; *"honey, when I saw this double door refrigerator in red, I knew I had to get it for you"*. Sounds familiar? You are actually trying to convince her that it is your love for her that made you buy this thing, yet it is your love for you that brought you to that decision.

What if she really wanted that refrigerator? you might ask. Let me tell you something, it doesn't matter how much she wanted that fridge, if you'd only done one more round in the shop you probably would have found something more personal that she could enjoy herself.

Whose food is going to be chilled in that refrigerator anyway? Oh, it's yours? So you are also benefiting from this very loving gift to your wife?

You are just deceiving yourself and demonstrating the most selfish elements in you at the very moment when your love is meant to shine. Many men actually think it's a win-win situation. I mean think about it, the old fridge needs replacing and at the same time the wife's birthday is around the corner. Talk about killing two birds with one stone.

I call that one a 419 birthday present, you buy yourself a present and just put someone else's name on the package so that you make yourself feel good about your 'generosity'. If you were following this revelation that's what we would call a KAKOS present.

Many believers in church are doing the same to the Lord, you will be surprised to find out that some of them are reading this book right now.

They will swear on their lives that they have given and yet God is not responding, but when you zero in on their sacrifice you will find out that it was actually a 419 sacrifice or SHAVED OFF one. It was designed to dupe the one receiving the gift into thinking that it was for them yet it was a 'selfie'. That kind of giving can never back up your prayer, you are still speaking empty words before God. There are no reserves to back up your words in prayer.

You walk out of church feeling like you have you just carried the cross of Christ and should be canonized, when all you have done is pay rent for the church that month. Don't get me wrong it's not that what you pay in church rent is little, no. The question we need to address is who gets to enjoy the church building after the rent is paid for? It's you right?! So then you can't turn around and say; *'yes Lord look at what I have done for you?'* Unless you are paying rent for somebody else's church then you have just paid your own rent and are now trying to present it as a gift to God.

It's got a 419 sacrifice written all over it.

Deception of a gift

Imagine how you would react if your own son decided that he and the rest of the family were going to celebrate and honour you on your birthday. He invites everybody you care about and his speech about how much you mean to the family and what a wonderful father you are has everyone in tears. That is right up until you get to the gift he got for you, you are blindfolded and led through the kitchen into the garage.

This is a very proud moment for any father all your friends and colleagues are there to witness this occasion. The blindfold comes off and right in the corner is a shiny, brand new red scooter. Your 17 year-old son looks at you with so much pride and says; 'daddy look at what we got for you, it's a brand new car! Now I don't have to take the bus to school I can use this.'

He didn't buy you a gift, he just bought himself one in your name! That is exactly what believers are doing to God and wonder why they have nothing backing up their prayers. Many right now will testify of how much they have given but it seems as if God treats different the sacrifices that come from different people. This is far from the truth.

Acts 10: 34
Then Peter opened his mouth, and said, of a truth I perceive that God is no respecter of persons:

Now I want you to consider this carefully, if the money you gave for your church rent or a sound system becomes your sacrifice or offering that means you're benefiting from it right?

So in other words, God has just bought you a sound system with the offering you gave. He has just paid the church rent for you.

It's the same thing with what some of those believers who are reading this book do when it comes to tithes and offerings. The day the preacher teaches on the importance of tithing on that day you will record the highest tithe but the offering figures will be on an all-time low. What happened? They just diverted what they normally give as offering to tithe so that they are 'covered' when it comes to the tithe that the preacher has just spoken of. The truth of the matter is that they have not given a penny more than what they normally do.

Their hearts were not changed one bit by what they heard, instead they just tried to cover what they know they are doing wrong. That money you used to buy a mic for the choir cannot be your sacrifice and cannot back up your medium of exchange when it comes to prayer.

You are the one who enjoys the music when they sing who do you think should pay for that? If you give that mic as your sacrifice, then God has just bought you a microphone for the choir. How can that then build a memorial for your prayer?

You are now receiving the sacrifice yourself. It no longer has the ability to become the backing to your medium of exchange. As a result, you are still praying **kakos** (amiss) you have deviated from the prescribed way to pray. Your prayer before God still appears as the prayer of a heathen, when unbelievers pray they are speaking empty words to God. They have no grounds to even approach him.

Back in the old testament if you brought your offering, the moment you handed it to the priest it would automatically change its essence. If you just touched it after giving it, you would die immediately. You have just touched something that is holy that doesn't belong to you.

I mean this could be your goat that you brought from home the moment you hand it over to God and that priest accepts it, it now belongs to God. Touching it after that was the same thing as you going into the holy of holies and taking from there some of the holy ornaments that were sacred and were only to be used by the priesthood. The consequences were the same, you would die immediately.

That is the reason why Ananias died. He took for himself the same thing he had given to God. I strongly advise against it. So you can't claim that the thing you bought for your own use is for God. You will still be frustrated in your prayer life, there is nothing backing your prayer.

Now I don't want to lose you in this final chapter as I reveal the heart of God concerning prayer this truth changed my life.

Chapter 8

Obedience Better than Scarifice

In the midst of a scathing indictment against King Saul's presumption and arrogance, the prophet Samuel utters these famous words,

1 Samuel 15: 22
And Samuel said, hath the Lord great delight in burnt offerings and sacrifices, as in obeying the voice of the Lord? Behold to obey is better than sacrifice, and to heed is better than the fat of rams.

I know we have already covered a great deal on the subject of prayer and how to get God's attention in these previous chapters but if you miss what I'm about to show you in this last chapter, you have lost the whole plot. I need you to follow very closely because we are getting ready to delve deeper into what God really expects of you.

Saul's great, heroic idea

Saul had heard the word of the Lord, but thought he had a better idea. He was supposed to destroy the Amalekites completely, taking no plunder, but instead he spared the best of the sheep and cattle.

"to sacrifice to the Lord."

This might seem like a noble gesture on Saul's part, wanting to sacrifice to the Lord... so why does Samuel make such a big deal out of this? **Why is obedience so much better than sacrifice?**

Sacrifice means independence from God

In this sense it's actually an attempt to gain independence from God. If we sacrifice for him, then we have put him in our debt. If we sacrifice for God, he owes us something (or so we think). You are now using sacrifice is a way of "buying" whatever you want to get from God (protection, deliverance, provision, favour), while at the same time remaining independent from him.

For you to sacrifice means that you have given something of value to you for the sake of other considerations. A sacrifice costs you something, a good example we came across in the previous chapters is the Moabite king who sacrificed his eldest son. It was a sacrifice because he couldn't go down the market and buy himself another son, it cost him dearly to give up his son.

That was a sacrifice, and yes it is your seed or sacrifice that backs up the prayer you make in the secret place and gives value to the words you are speaking. As good as that sounds, the religious mind has already devised a way to make it an unpleasant thing in the eyes of the Lord. Saul found himself in this very same place and many of God's people are sacrificing to no avail and continue to be frustrated because it seems as if they have done their part but God just won't do his.

The church has managed to change the sacrifice from what God meant it to be. I know right now many of you reading this are guilty of doing the same thing.

Have you ever messed up in a big way, and after that something bad happens to you? You almost feel as if its ok for that bad thing to come your way, because it makes you feel justified for your wrong. It's as if the attitude is, now I have paid the price and I think we are all good with God now.

Every time you miss the mark you are always looking for something you can do to make up for it, your sacrifice is no longer for God but for you. I know I have a lot of witnesses out there.

That sister at church who sings with you in the choir and is not even as faithful as you are in attending practice, all of sudden the news of her engagement comes to your hearing. You had the same prayer request, but you are still waiting and you begin to question God on how come she gets it first when you are more faithful, or you give more that she does? You have just fallen into the same trap, you have just forgotten the reason why God demands a sacrifice.

It's like a woman once said to Tim Keller, upon realizing the gospel for the first time,

"I know why I want my morality to save me. If I'm saved by my good works, then like a taxpayer, I have rights. I've paid into the system and God owes me a good and decent life. And there is a limit to what the Father can ask of me. But if I'm saved by sheer grace, then my life belongs entirely to the Father, he owes me nothing and there is no limit to what he can ask of me."

"God, look at all I've done for you! You owe me this, it's only fair!" we say.

We demand our goodies from God, but we retain our right to do what we want with our lives. We just need to make sure we throw a few sacrifices God's way every once in a while to keep him at bay. This is the attitude of sacrifice that Saul personified. It is not God's way.

The life of sacrifice is a life of demanding my rights and living as I wish. The life of obedience, though, is a response to God's gracious invitation and is lived as an upward spiral of dependence and intimacy.

Obedience is dependent trust in God

The time, place and manner of a sacrifice can be usually determined ahead of time, and often by us. A sacrifice can often be a matter of our own choice and will. This is rarely, if ever, true of obedience. Sacrifice can be a matter of our initiative. Obedience is always a matter of our response to God's initiative. Obedience may require sacrifice, but Saul's sacrifice was not an act of obedience

Behold to obey is better than sacrifice, and to heed is better than the fat of rams.

The words of Samuel rocked Saul's world and turned it the right side up, up to this point his concept of sacrifice was wrong. He was convinced he had done the right thing but in doing so failed the ultimate test. Let me break it down for you.

If I said to you today give to me 5% of every penny you will receive this year, it's a lot for some but most people will be able to get by just fine with 5 percent less of what they normally have. If you follow my instruction you have obeyed me, you have submitted to me in your obedience. If I turn around and said to you, I want 90 percent of everything you are going to make this year, that's a whole different ball game. Your obedience and submission is now being tested at a whole new level. Its huge sacrifice for most to give away 90 percent of all you earn, now you are sacrificing in obedience.

Your sacrifice is now proof of your submission and obedience to the one who commanded you to do it. Nearly everyone can do the 5 percent but the 90 percent takes an individual who has already made up their mind that whatever God asks I will do. This is what makes a sacrifice meaningful to God, the widow of Zarephath found herself in the same position.

God was demanding all she had when she needed it herself, she had nothing to spare.

1 Kings 17: 12
And she said, as the Lord thy God liveth, I have not a cake, but an handful of meal in a barrel, and a little oil in a cruse and, behold, I am gathering two sticks, that I may go in and dress it for me and my son, that we may eat it and die.

Obedience, is the response of someone who is in a relationship of trust with God. We trust God, we depend on him, we are interactive with him, but he takes the lead. Obedience is better than sacrifice because we are letting God be God and staying in our proper place with him, the place of dependence and surrender to his goodness.

This is why Jesus didn't say,

"If you love me, sacrifice for me."

Instead he said,

"Anyone who loves me will obey my teaching. My Father will love them, and we will come to them and make our home with them."

This kind of obedience is a response to divine love always leads to intimacy and dependence. **This is why obedience is better than sacrifice.** Notice that this verse doesn't say 'don't sacrifice' It is simply showing you what's more important than the other and also showing you how obedience can't exist without sacrifice. There is no obedience without sacrifice although there can be sacrifice without obedience.

Obedience is better than sacrifice but you can never come to the place of obedience apart from the grace of God and the apostle Paul spelt it out so beautifully in his letter to the Philippian church.

Philippians 2: 13
For it is God which worketh in you both to will and to do of his good pleasure.

God is already working in you right now to bring you to that place were you are flowing with his perfect will for your life. There are things that God has put in place to prosper you and by his grace he works in you to bring you into his perfect plan. He is all too aware of the fact that you cannot do it without him. That is the reason why he delights in your sacrifice it spells your total surrender and dependency on him alone.

Paul had looked at his own successes and could see the hand of God all over him as he testified in his letter to the Corinthians;

1 Corinthians 15: 10
But by the grace of God I am what I am and his grace which was bestowed upon me was not in vain; but I laboured more abundantly than they all: yet not I, but the grace of God which was with me.

God himself is the author of true obedience and sacrifice. Paul was mightily used by God but instead of telling us how good he was he points us once more to the grace. But then he says something interesting right there. He says;

"but I laboured more abundantly than they all,"

Now wait a minute Paul has already told us that he is who he is because of the grace of God but then he seems to make a U-turn when he says;" I laboured".

He is addressing one of the biggest issues in Christianity as we know it today. Paul is pointing you to the fact that if you had observed him working his way in ministry and in life in general you would have been impressed. But then he turns around and says;

"yet not I but the grace of God which was with me."

In other words, when Paul would obey God and present his sacrifices that was the grace of God working to position him to receive every promise of God. Paul actually knew that you could have looked at the things that he had and actually think it was all him, yet God himself was at work to causing him to walk in obedience, that's the good news we preach.

Do you see how simple this is, God says;

"obedience is better than sacrifice"

Then tells you that through the Good News of His grace he is going to empower you to do just that. I know, its nearly too good to true, it is the same thing as being told you are going to sit an exam, but then the invigilator turns around and says; *"don't worry I will also provide the answers with the questions."*

The things you would have observed Paul doing as works were a manifestation of the grace that was working in him, Hallelujah! Grace is not a licence to be lazy, it makes you do, it causes you to act in the way you ought to.

Paul is saying that if you had looked at him with the eye of the flesh, you would have seen him ticking every box in the natural. He was the kind of brother that comes early to set up the sound system at church and is always the last one to leave because they are cleaning up after everybody else.

What seed constitutes sacrifice and obedience

Right now you are a warehouse of seeds, your smile is a seed, your time is a seed and sometimes even just lending a hand to someone in need is a seed. The reason why God demands money is because it means the most to you so your greatest sacrifice will come in the form of money. God is after the thing you don't want to give him the most and that he sees as the ultimate sacrifice and obedience.

However, the sacrifice and obedience you would have seen would have stemmed from God himself, He is the one who works in you to bring you to the place of obedience.

Understand that it is when your sacrifice and obedience is of your own human effort that you miss the mark or as they say in archery you sin. Paul says in all that, it was the grace of God working through him. He was sacrificing in obedience fully dependant of the Lord. This is where many are missing it.

You need to know that it is the will of God to answer every prayer you utter; he wants to grant the desires of your heart. When you kneel down to pray by his grace he is already working in your heart to give, so that whatever you utter in prayer secures the answer you need.

God wants you to know how to access every blessing that he has made available to you as a believer when you pray. Your prayer now becomes the effectual fervent prayer of a righteous man; you are now praying the prayer that God has to answer.

The Conclusion

In a nutshell, you set a *seed* aside before you pray and let your seed be the value of your prayer. You may ask how much? But as I showed you in the previous chapter the Lord said of the woman who gave two mites;

"she gave all she could."

Give *all you can* and that stands as the value behind your prayer and that prayer is *the prayer God can't ignore*.

Open yourself to that revelation whatever church you attend and you will arrest the attention of heaven and like Cornelius you will be endowed with the same power to disturb God's attention with your memorial rising before him and obstructing his view from the splendour of heaven. You will with his permission and his own obedience to his word, 'force' the power of heaven to locate you.

I have employed this prayer ever since and taught my close associates in business and in Christendom to use it effectively and they have been seeing undeniable results. I have many millionaires around me and many people receiving breakthrough after breakthrough through this formidable prayer. This has been my secret for a long time and I had never felt the Lord saying I should reveal it to the greater public until now.

I have seen the Lord's hand in my life time and time again through this prayer and you too can join me in this revelation that yields results as we pray **THE PRAYER THAT GOD CAN'T IGNORE!**

Lightning Source UK Ltd.
Milton Keynes UK
UKHW020605090719
345839UK00005B/1179